Exposing the SHOCKING Truth
in Letters from Satan on
CHILDHOOD SEXUAL ABUSE

C.W. Fossett

Detroit, MI, USA

Thanks for Everything! Exposing the SHOCKING Truth in Letters from Satan on CHILDHOOD SEXUAL ABUSE
Copyright © 2016 C.W. Fossett

All scripture quotations, unless otherwise indicated, are taken from the HOLY BIBLE, KING JAMES VERSION and are marked (KJV).

Scripture quotations marked (NLT) are taken from the *Holy Bible*, New Living Translation, copyright ©1996, 2004, 2007, 2013 by Tyndale House Foundation. Used by permission of Tyndale House Publishers, Inc., Carol Stream, Illinois 60188. All rights reserved.

Scripture quotations from THE MESSAGE. Copyright © by Eugene H. Peterson 1993, 1994, 1995, 1996, 2000, 2001, 2002. Used by permission of Tyndale House Publishers, Inc.

All rights reserved. No part of this publication may be reproduced, stored in a retrieval system, or transmitted in any form or by any means – electronic, mechanical, photocopy, recording, or any other – except for brief quotations in printed reviews, without the prior permission of the publisher.

NOTE: The author acknowledges that correctly written English capitalizes all proper nouns. However, throughout this work all references to the person of satan are not capitalized as a display of Christ's triumph over him.

*Priority*ONE Publications
P. O. Box 34722 • Detroit, MI 48234
E-mail: info@priorityonebooks.com
URL: http://www.priorityonebooks.com

ISBN 13:   978-1-933972-39-8
ISBN 10:   1-933972-39-4

Edited by Patricia A. Hicks
Cover and Interior design by Christina Dixon

Printed in the United States of America

Dedication

This book is dedicated to the one person that I put over my pain; I did not want you to hurt like me. I know you loved me and did your best for me; I miss you Fanny.

I also dedicate this book to all the hurting children, even if now grown. It was not your fault. We did not deserve to be treated that way. We are precious and strong, not weak. We are precious, not dirty. Even though we have been raped in the past, we will not allow the rape of our future. We are able to grow past the pain and heal.

Why? Because God is willing, and we are worth the process to heal!

To my two girls who had to endure all my fears and anxieties coming up as children to being my biggest cheerleaders.

To my sisters who have prayed me through this whole process.

To Mr. Fossett who nurtured and protected my five-year-old girl inside and kept my secrets and shared my pain.

Preface

It's time to wake up and heal. So often we think that time heals all wounds. That is not true. For too many of us, the wound from rape and molestation has festered, become infected, and now it is septic and in critical condition. It's time to take a good look at where we as adults go wrong and see how we have willingly been played by the enemy, fell for his tricks, and lost too much in the process. Maybe, if we hear from satan himself, we can get a clue and change.

Before we start reading, let us pray because only GOD can help us look at ourselves, heal, and change.

Believers:
Father God, please help me to open my heart to hear what is being said in these pages. Lord, please allow me to hear, repent, heal, and change. I know I can't do anything without You. I don't want to do anything without You. Help me Lord, give me ears to hear. Help me not to harden my heart, because I know if I do, it will keep me away from You, in a place of darkness. In Jesus' name I pray, Amen.

Non-believers:
God please show me myself. Help me to know that if I'm not Yours I am his. Help me read these pages and see how satan

works so I will long for You, believe in You, confess all of my sins, and follow You, Amen.

Contents

Dedication .... *i*
Preface .... *iii*
satan Speaks – An Introduction 7
Letters from satan
   1.   The Younger the Better 9
   2.   Deadbeat Dads 10
   3.   Keep it in the Family..12
   4.   Little Secrets 14
   5.   Thanks for Throwing Them Away 16
   6.   There's No People Like Church People 18
   7.   The Gift That Keeps on Giving.............................20
   8.   It Only Takes a Minute..22
   9.   Boys are Precious Too 23
  10.   Expect the One You Least Expect 25
  11.   It's All You Girl 27
  12.   Just Lines in a Movie...28
  13.   Generational Curses 30
  14.   Think About It 32
  15.   Hit Me Up 33
  16.   New Recruits...34
  17.   Shout Out 36

18. So Good You Can't Just Have One – Yum 38
19. No Need to Thank Me 39
20. PTSD..41
21. Busy, Busy..42
22. All in the Family 43
23. Can't Say it Enough 44
24. Ask Me a Question and I Will Tell You a Lie 45
25. Smoke Screen..47
26. Not My Man..48
27. Dear Old Dad 50
28. My Boy 51
29. Johnny Come Lately 52
30. There's Room for You..53

Cathy's Cry 55
C.W.'s Mission..57
C.W. Speaks..59
The Shephard Speaks 63
Pick a Side 64
My Story..68
Only GOD 71
God's Love Letter...77
Precious Blood Prayer...82
About the Author...83

satan Speaks – An Introduction

This book is a series of thank you letters from me (satan) to all adults who make it so easy for me to kill, steal, and destroy all the little children in your care.

Thank you so much! If it had not been for all of your help, I would not have been able to enjoy all the wonderful moments that will keep giving to me and to you and yours. You make it so easy for me I just have to take time to write all of you that make it so easy for me to spend time with your young daughters, granddaughters, nieces, grand nieces, and we can't forget all of your sons. The boys not only are gifts to me from you but they love to pass the gift along to other people's daughters too. That makes me so happy. It motivates me to continue my devious work.

Jesus Christ even spoke about me. His disciple recorded His commentary in St. John 10:10 (KJV), "The thief cometh not, but for to steal, and to kill, and to destroy…" But, you just couldn't believe Him.

Letter No. 1
The Younger the Better

To all you young moms out there, sleeping around having baby after baby, looking for love on your back because of what your uncle did when you were five, thanks so much! You know why? Because after just a few years you start to feel cheated. You let your guard down and you get in that "what about me" phase. It's like Christmas that lasts all year. You're just so selfish toward your babies. I just can't stop giving it to them. A parent's pain and inconvenience is all my pleasure.

So, one big thanks to all you not thinking, unprotected sex-havers, what-about-me phasers, don't know who my baby's daddy is, and want more on my bridge card heifers – keep up the good work! If you are a "going to the clinic" kind of girl, you work for me by giving me more to work with. Thank you! There's nothing like killing your baby. The shame, regret, and emptiness of heart, mind, and soul keeps you working for me and on a good day you want to ride the suicide express. I understand. You have had it hard. No one cared for you. So, when a man gives you the tiniest bit of time, he wants you, and he loves you, right? Can you hear me laughing? There's this game I play. I bait you until you give in, and when you do, I make you feel bad for doing it. Then I coax you into doing it again. You can call it misery merry-go-round; want to ride?

Letter No. 2

Deadbeat Dads

This letter is for all the deadbeat Dads that don't have time; especially when it's due to investing time in making more children for me to love on. Thank you for not being there. Thank you for not calling. Thank you for thinking that paying $20 dollars a week is enough fathering for you. Thank you for letting your girlfriend answer your cell phone when your children call, lying and saying that you're not there. Thank you for not showing up for any programs or award ceremonies. Thanks for not playing ball with your boys and having tea with your girls.

And then this is my favorite thanks! Thanks for missing birthday after birthday and not even sending a gift or a card. Hell, you didn't even call. That opened the door for me to invest $50 dollars, and he was asking for a sleep over? I have a bad rep. Yes, I steal, kill, and destroy. But you just make my job so easy. It's almost as if you gift wrap them and have them delivered first class.

Thanks for holding on to all that bitterness from not having a dad yourself or the excuse of, "How am I supposed to know how to be a dad when I never had one?" Hell, you didn't even try. Thank you, thank you, thank you for blaming that b _ _ _ _ for trapping you. Your attitude is a gift that keeps on giving. Thanks dawg, good lookin' out.

P.S. – Doing more for your girlfriend's babies than your own gives your children the gift of a lifetime supply of bitterness and gaps for my workers to step in and give them all the love you wouldn't. Thanks again.

Letter No. 3

Keep it in the Family

"I have never let my children go to daycare! If family can't watch them, I don't have to go." This is a door I've entered in many, many times. It's right up there with,

"Oh, where are the kids?"

"They're fine. They are with their uncle watching TV."

I'm not like HIM. I can't be everywhere at the same time, so I have workers. You know them as your brother, nephew, or boyfriends – who are not even family (and hasn't even made any real commitment to you). All because you make it so easy, and he's so willing. Oh yeah, I can't forget the one you never expected, little RJ. He's only a few years older, so he tends to fly under the radar; not to mention, he took the babysitters class.

Don't forget cousin so & so's foster daughter. She just had to try what was done to her; only this time she wants to be the one in charge. I won't forget your sons either. They walk around quiet, afraid, confused, and/or angry, and they no longer trust anybody; not even HIM – priceless.

Somehow you never seem to notice the change in them, never. When they grow up and start to self-destruct, it's a win, win situation – for me. Before long, he's taking all that pent-up anger out on everyone everywhere. The more he hurts, the more he hurts others. The more I hurt him, the more he touches the little boy down the street, or she touches the little girl in the bathroom at church, and they can't even look at themselves in the mirror for weeks let alone have a good relationship. There is nothing like passing on the pain. I thank you and your family, too.

Letter No. 4

Little Secrets

Thanks for not talking about things and keeping it all a secret. Thanks for all those nights sleeping in your closet. Thanks for being too hurt to pray. Thanks for all those feelings just building and building inside you.

Bitterness is my playground. The church has nothing for you except sermons laced with my favorite line, **"Get over it!"** It's just fuel for the fire. That fire is fueled by unforgiveness, keeping quiet, or when the family knows what's happening (like King David in the Bible - 2 Samuel 13); but the beat goes on and they still choose to do nothing – nothing effective anyway. Years later I stole her childhood, or killed his desire to be with women, or made momma feel guilty. It's the gift that keeps on giving.

I had this one girl beg her whole family to keep quiet so her momma wouldn't be hurt by any details. She was an amusement park of pain. By holding it in for years, she made herself sick. Wanna know the bonus? After he used her like a nasty jack off rag, her aunt made her sit at the tub for hours scrubbing his stains out of her panties. When her momma died, he even spoke at the funeral at the very church where he bothered her in the basement; right near where the repast table was set. When she finally confronted him, he was too saved to ask for forgiveness. I still got him too. He keeps his secrets and hers real good.

Secrets are a pressure cooker of pain; they just keep simmering all the hurt, tears, and insecurities. Sshhhhhh, don't tell anybody. It's our little secret.

Letter No. 5

Thanks for Throwing Them Away

Some of your children I had to steal. Some of you just gave them to me. You know your teens; the ones that know everything, with all the mouth, rolling their eyes, wanting attention so bad that they would tear up your family to prove a point? That point is almost always something small that you parents didn't notice, missed, overlooked, or just didn't take the time to investigate. When they said something to you about this hurt, you took offense instead of asking them to forgive you for neglecting them. Thanks for adding fuel to the fire.

All parties involved are just feeling ignored and unloved. A neglected child is my favorite kind of child. There are so many of them. Thanks for throwing them away. Thanks for taking his word over your own daughter's. Thanks for thinking your job is done when they're thirteen. Thanks for not praying with them or for them. Thanks for not taking them to church. Thanks for bringing all my workers into your house. Your children were on display like a tasty buffet. Thanks for not teaching them to avoid my workers. Thanks for treating your little man different because he got a different daddy. Thanks for letting them spend the night. Thanks for being caught up in and with drinking, smoking, sexin', everything, and everybody else. You know, all your help me outs that trained her to get set up, and then tore up from the floor up as an excellent candidate for my workers to take. Thanks!

Letter No. 6
There's No People Like Church People

Thanks so much to all you "church people." Even after you found out I stole your daughter's innocence, killed her joy, and destroyed your son's future of what it could have been, your response raped them again. When you were more worried about ruining your ministry, what the people at the church would think, or how your how your out-of-wedlock child could do this to you, you were playing right into my hands. You had already left them alone by going to every service and not missing one thing, except your child's birthday, school program, or when they were sick. Thank you for neglecting your first ministry.

People love to talk about the crack mommas giving their daughters to the crack man. But nobody talks about good Sis. Sue pimpin' her daughter out to Deacon Can't Get Right and her sons to Minister Let Me Blow Your Horn of Music. Thank you for spending more time witnessing in the streets than at home. Thanks for spending your bill money on keeping up appearances that will pay off more than you know. Your children will resent the church for years. The resulting bitterness, along with unforgiveness, is like a four-layer cake. And you not admitting that you were wrong? That is the icing.

Thanks for sitting in church all those years and not getting it, but you know the "Word." Thank your pastor for me. The fact that he didn't preach one sermon on family being your first ministry helps me. For many of you, the only sermon you heard about children was spare the rod and spoil the child. There were no sermons on protecting your family from rapists or molesters. Nor was there effective teaching on the power of forgiveness or growing past the pain. How precious.

Didn't you know pastors work for me too? No one is exempt. Not one. Not even you. If you read this and don't change or ask your pastor to expound on these subjects, you're working for me too. Thanks in advance.

Letter No. 7
The Gift that Keeps on Giving

To all the adults that have held our time together a secret for all these years. For whatever reason, you've been too scared to let it out. You are like me reliving it over and over again. Your body reacts as if it's happening for the first time, making your blood pressure rise, and ulcers form; not to mention all those wonderful mental disorders.

Thanks for not sharing our secret about your body with anyone – making me your first and last. Thanks for not sharing with your husband why you pull away; he thinks it's him. And for the men, you know your wife will never look at you the same. People think I only prey on girls. Not so. Little boys really don't tell. When they hold it in, their very manhood is in question. When my worker is a man, they think they are gay. When it's a woman (yes, I have women workers), the little boy's trust is totally scrambled up. Often, he becomes one of my workers. He passes the love to his mom's friend's children, his nieces or nephews, and maybe his own brothers and sisters that he babysits – using all the tricks that were used on him.

Thanks for not getting help or saying anything. You allowed so many after you to get the same attention. Thanks for being mad at HIM but not getting any comfort from the Father, Son, and Holy Ghost for that matter. Thanks for being so lost in your pain that you can't move past it; nor can you help anybody else. Quiet people are not a threat to me. They actually please me very much. Shhhh…keep holding it in. When you do, you work for me. For that I am thankful. Good looking out!

Letter No. 8
It Only Takes a Minute

Thanks to all you parents that believe that as long as my child never spends the night or doesn't spend time with people you don't know means that they are safe. You check on your babies after 30 minutes or an hour. My workers are trained to get in, do damage, and keep on movin'. It only takes a minute to change a life. How long do think it takes to fondle someone's future away? It only takes a moment to turn them from sweet to sour – quick stick or lick – all done. I do what I got to do in a hurry. You're worried about hours. All I need is moments. I fondled one little girl behind a curtain with her momma on the other side after her grandmother's funeral.

Grief is a good distraction. So is death, heartbreak, loss of a job, got a new man (or woman), or playing around with an old flame. That's all me and my workers need. You think, "But I can't be with her every minute." I like you kind of mommas. Truth be told, most of the time you didn't even check. Keep being caught up in your hurts and pains, please. The more you think it's about you, the more damage I can do to you and yours. Wait for it, wait for it…. Bingo! We just got another one. Now do you have a minute? No? That's okay, we do. Thanks so much.

Letter No. 9
Boys are Precious Too

Saying "thank you" is not enough. I should buy you a present for all the little boys you've given me. Most folks try to keep up with their girls. But the boys, just like money on the sidewalk, somebody's gonna get it. So, I get them too.

My women workers come in real handy. They are so nice. It doesn't matter if they are young or old, big or little, light or dark, they've got y'all fooled. When people find out a boy is sexually active they just think he started early not realizing that his ability to be intimate has just been distorted. He doesn't trust his momma. After all, she let it happen. When he gets older, all I have to do is send a little aggressive thang over to him and he folds like a card table. I should buy you two gifts 'cause when he is feeling really lonely, I can send a man over to take care of him. He'll never be the same again. His daddy ain't around, if you know who he is. The man you're with, he shouldn't be around you let alone your kids.

That's the problem with you parents; you act like boys aren't precious to me. By not protecting your boys, not caring who you bring around, and not suspecting women, all your poor choices are gifts to me. That's why I should give you something special, not just years of hurt and pain. That's nothing. Not just tears and fears; I give that out every day.

Maybe if I whisper, "You're better off dead." Now that's the perfect gift. Nothing says thank you like making your boy's funeral arrangements.

Are they precious to you yet?

Letter No. 10
Expect the One You Least Expect

As if only old and ugly people work for me, you never suspect my workers who are close to you. If I had a payroll, everybody would be getting paid. You know them, but you don't really know them. You let your guard down 'cause they're your brother or sister, neighbor or friend. The fact that you know these people makes it even better for me because you are looking for a stranger, not a friend – let alone family.

Just think my people work for free. I don't even give them a promise like HIM.

"She's so nice, I met her at church. She's a pretty young lady and she's good with my boys. She goes above and beyond what I expect."

"He's such a good young man; he took the babysitting class. He's certified. He's Dorothy Lou's son, and you know they are just like family."

This is my favorite set up – the one you least expect. You never suspect it, and when you find out, it's a two for one rape. You're watching your girls and not your boys, your teens but not your babies. You think I'm only attracted to the poor, black, or dumb. Not so. I like them all; rich, poor, black, white, in between, and on the side. No one is exempt; I like them all.

You fail to check her because of one of my biggest lies – only men molest kids. Keep thinking,

"He's a boy so he liked it."

"He's like one of the family." "He would never ever. No, not him."

Thanks to me, your son doesn't like it, Sister Dorothy's son would, and you don't have a clue. Win, win for team satan. Thanks. Your ignorance is a gift that keeps on giving, and I thank you all with a familiar face to boot.

Letter No. 11

It's All You Girl

Thank you so much for working all those long hours so you can get your nails and hair done. It's hard being a single mom. But you know what they say,

"You do what you got to do to take care of me, myself, and I."

"Oh yeah, I meant the kids, too."

Thank you for working all that overtime! The fact that after work you are "sooo tired" has opened many doors for me to slide right in to lend a helping hand. Everybody needs help from time to time, right? It reminds me of the time you came home from work and asked one of my workers to watch the kids so you could unwind and take a bath. You know me, anything to lend a hand. That was the first time, I had already softened up the kids with ice cream, chips, and a little Nick Jr. Most importantly, you were too busy to give them what they wanted most – you.

Thank you. You think it's only about you – not the kids. I do all the work and you get all the credit. I don't mind. It's the least I can do since you've given me so much.

Letter No. 12

Just Lines in a Movie

Just when you think Sophia is just talking junk in the classic movie, *Color Purple*...

"All my life I had to fight. I had to fight my daddy. I had to fight my uncles. I had to fight my brothers. A girl child ain't safe in a family of men, but I ain't never thought I'd have to fight in my own house!"

Did you hear of two brothers molesting their younger sisters? You didn't know I recycle? The boys got molested, then kept silent or ignored; so now they want to share all of that attention. Who do you think they want to share with – that fast tail girl down the street? Nope. What about the fast girl at school, or even at church? Noooooooooooooo! If you can't molest the one you want, molest your little sisters. There's no breast like the ones down the hall. Talk about keeping it all in the family. There's no need to thank me. Thank you for being so willing to damage a sibling. My tricks worked on Cain too. Siblings got to love them. There's nothing like making y'all think you can't trust anybody – not even your brothers or sisters.

I think your momma said it best,

"You just do whatever comes to your crazy mind!"

Oh, my bad. What she really said was,

"Don't do everything that comes to your crazy mind!"

Same thang! It's a few words that are different, right?

Letter No. 13
Generational Curses

I just can't get enough of my spiritual puppets. They talk about HIM. But they refuse to talk about when grandma was almost raped by a man that woke her up with money in hand and a willing body; or when auntie was molested, and now your brother is her brother too; not to mention how you and now your niece have been violated. Man oh man, you all love to jump on that good old generational curse.

It's not a curse. It's just my dedicated workers. They have been following your family and compiling data from years past. And they will keep gathering information and using it against your family for years to come.

You're so spiritual. Even I know you need more than catch phrases and two scriptures. Even my newest workers know that. You're so spiritual you forgot all about HIM. Believe it or not, HE was there for grandma, auntie and nem and anybody else in the family. How many times will it take for you people to understand I came to steal, kill, and destroy? So, if I get just half a chance to steal your faith in HIM before it grows, I will.

If I can rape you of your confidence and kill and destroy any chance of you and yours of getting past the pain so that you can keep blaming HIM for it all, I will. It's just that plain and simple.

I have, and I will continue my crafty work down your family line. No need to thank me. I'm happy to oblige.

Letter No. 14

Think About It

Do you think I'm only out to destroy one life? Unlike HIM I'm on a group plan. Only HE does the true intimate one-on-one. You've got to understand your child is just for starters. From there grows the guilt of the parents, grandparents, aunties, not to mention my workers, top it off with the child's future mate; straight or gay I don't discriminate. And the cherry on top is the child's children. Nothing says thank you like screwing up the next generation.

My fun is stealing hope, killing dreams, destroying any chance of a relationship with HIM. Do you know why I don't have a problem with telling you just a few of my secrets? Because you don't change even after you hear HIM it means nothing after you hear me. I figure, you don't want to change. Am I right?

No big secret here. The more you avoid the issues the deeper my roots go. And even though you are reading my words I'm not worried. Why should I? You read HIS words and don't change. So for that I say thanks.

Letter No. 15

Hit Me Up

Your lack of attention has opened many doors!

No, I mean open many web pages for me to do what I do. My workers and I are high tech these days. We do it all. They'll hit you up on facebook, and MySpace is your space. Also Twitter and video chatting should have my name on it. Who do you think started sexting?

I got them right where I want them, and you don't even set up parental controls or check on them.

P.S. - Thanks for paying the bill though.

Letter No. 16

New Recruits

I'll recruit anybody, not just momma's boyfriend, your uncle, the man at the church, or the woman at school. Hell, I'll use your goddaddy, granddaddy, step-daddy, and your momma too. Why not? Everybody is too scared to get in anybody's business.

Although they see the signs and talk about it behind your back, they just look away. If somebody does say something to them, they just go off on them and make them out to be the bad guy. Then, when it's all said and done, I've just recruited the child, their parents, and all y'all good look away-ers. Thanks for looking away.

There are the daddies that just can't stop noticing how much his daughter is shaped just like her momma was back in the day and that momma just don't do the things she used to in order to please. Believe me, not every momma is a saint, especially the one that makes her son give her a bath – some mommas are just so dirty.

Look away. Look away, oh ah oh, thanks for the dance.

1 John 3:8a King James Version (KJV)
⁸"He that committeth sin is of the devil; for the devil sinneth from the beginning."

1 John 3:8a (The Message)
"Those who make a practice of sin are straight from the Devil, the pioneer in the practice of sin."

Letter No. 17

Shout Out

I want to give a shout out to all my workers – some you know and some of you don't. Let's get to it:

- Momma's boyfriend, especially the one who hates her kids
- Uncles
- That school teacher
- The little league coach
- The piano player from church
- Sister Sue's son
- Auntie's foster child
- The momma that didn't want her son to go to jail
- The 15-year-old boy
- The 16-year-old girl
- The brother that notices his sister's changing body
- That youth pastor at church
- That counselor at the youth center
- The momma that has no time for her kids
- The daddy that is working on wife number three or four
- The neighbor who looks away when she see the signs

- The teacher that sees the signs and second guesses the situation
- The grandmother that refuses to believe that her son is bothering his step-son
- The daddy that caught his wife making their son give her a bath and just took over for him and did not say a word
- Your best friend's son
- The foster child you wanted to help but did not watch, let alone raise
- The parent that does not check on the kids playing because they are glad things are quiet for a change
- The person that you least expect
- Any person that don't believe in HIM, works for me
- The person that reads this book and does nothing to help protect the children in their care

Letter No. 18

So Good You Can't Have Just One - Yum

Thanks to all my workers that had to double back with that same child. Don't forget my worker that tried and liked it and just had to keep working on the kids you don't protect. It's like potato chips, you can't eat just one. You have to keep it going.

Candidates for employment with Satan are considered without regard to their race, color, religion, national origin, age, sex, gender, pregnancy, disability, sexual orientation, gender identity, genetic information, military status.

Letter No. 19

No Need to Thank Me

To all you wounded children that are now adults and have spent time and time again with my workers, there is no need to say thank you for your years of bitterness. Please allow me to continue using you by:

- Your smoking, drinking, and sleeping around
- Your ten abortions
- Your need to be loved at all cost
- Your willingness to work for me
- Your hateful disposition
- Your need to hurt everyone you come in contact with
- Your need to remind your parents how everything is their fault
- Your need to be angry with HIM
- Your need to sleep in your closet weekend after weekend
- Your need to stay invisible
- Your need to curl up in a ball for the rest of your life
- Your need to give up and give in
- Your need to play the blame game
- Your need to dibble and dabble in any and everything that comes your way

- Your need to give every child in your life that same attention my workers gave you
- Your need to break up your family
- Your need to play the blame game
- Your need to shut down, give up, and not try
- Your need to hate everyone that did nothing to save you, that could not or did not try to help a five-year-old girl, or a seven-year-old boy

Your need to self-destruct is thanks enough.

You're welcome!

Letter No. 20

PTSD

Nothing says thank you like a good case of PTSD. It's not a sexually transmitted disease, although that's good too. PTSD comes from people being in wars, people that have had to jump out of a burning building, people that have survived a deadly car, plane, or train crash, people that saw a crime in action, people that were shot, people that have had to bury their two-year-old girl after a drive-by, and people that have survived natural disasters. PTSD can also occur after one of my workers has spent some one-on-one time with your daughter, son, niece, nephew, little girl at church, the teen on the way home from school, the two-year-old girl that momma's boyfriend helped himself to and crushed her pelvis, the little boy at little league, the altar boy, the white, black, red, and yellow kid, the rich kids, poor kids, all in between kids, can have post-traumatic stress disorder.

It is a war going on. My workers and I are rounding up you and your kids. If you're not working for me, you're against me. Like I said, I'm not partial and no one is exempt.

Letter No. 21

Busy, Busy

Busy, busy, busy; work, work, work; gotta go, gotta go, gotta go; right now!

"Be good kids."

These words are music to my ears. I like it when you're so busy. Stay busy baby, keep workin'. Keep up the good work. Don't you gotta go right now? Go. Please go.

You people say you want babies so bad. But as soon as you do and they get to talking, you get to walking. You get so busy. Busy doing a bunch of nothing. Working and working with nothing to show for it.

You gotta goers, you got to go now, don't you? Go on. Leave your kids to me. Don't worry. I'll make sure they give you all the credit. You didn't know you were on my payroll; so just consider this as employee appreciation day. On second thought, let's make it a week. Thanks for all you do.

Letter No. 22

All in the Family

Thanks to my front line workers; the ones who are supposed to love, protect; and teach you. They bring new meaning to "daddy's little girl" and "momma's boy." Thank you daddy for all that one-on-one time with your little girl; showing her how much you really love her by rubbing her face and kissing her forehead before parting her thighs. Daddies like that make me so very proud. I can't forget the momma and her special boy having him practice on you so he'll be able to please his wife someday. Good job. And you wonder why the mental illness population is at an all-time high. You can thank me and my workers for that; no need though. The confusion in their minds is thanks enough.

Only HE gives a sound mind.

Letter No. 23

Can't Say it Enough

Thank you, Thank you, Gracias, Ahsante, grazie, Shukran, saha, merci, Arigato, Shakkran, Mh goi, Thanks awfully old boy, and Dankegon. I can't say it enough. I don't discriminate. It does not matter the race, age, origin, or size; my workers are equal opportunists. This is just a very small part of my children's division.

I have workers for every situation. Single, married, gay, straight, double back departments, and church people are the best people, just to name a few. I might tell you about my other divisions; it won't matter. You are not going to change. You want to hang out with me. I'm much more fun than HIM (or The Father, Son, and Holy Ghost). The only thing is HE has a better retirement plan than I do. You still have time. Come, let's just chill.

Letter No. 24
Ask Me a Question and I Will Tell You a Lie

Thanks to all you good questioning parents.

"Did somebody touch you?"

"Did he do this?"

"Did she do that?"

"Who?"

"What?"

Keep asking them. It's just what I would do. Questions are so much better than spending time observing them. You are way too busy for all of that. If something happens, at least you asked.

You can always let them know,

"If anybody touches you, I would go to jail cause I ain't having that! Not my babies!"

You people are so stupid and blind. You are so caught up in your crap you didn't notice the changes. Once an A student's grades go down, they start acting out. You think it's a phase and if my workers get in before they start school, you just think she's slow. Classic.

I have a question for you. How much are you willing to pay for my workers to stay away: time, attention, research? Never mind. You've got it covered. Thank you for asking.

Letter No. 25

Smoke Screen

Thank you for picking the wrong one to be "friends" with. Of all the children that my workers' pay special attention to, when the brave few tell you what's happening to them, you don't believe them. HE told you clear as day that I "come to kill, steal, and destroy."[1] I am determined to steal the truth, kill credibility, and destroy the child who is really telling the truth.

Think about it. Some of the people must be lying, right? I count on the fact that you won't believe it; not to mention your prejudice playing a part.

"That little black girl looked like she liked it."

"The little fast-tail white girl was asking for it."

People that think like that are why boys almost never tell. Hell, if they don't believe precious little girls, they are definitely not gonna believe horny little boys.

Thanks so much. Vacationing at my smoke screen resort; we pride ourselves in making wrong look right and right look wrong.

Come again, you hear?

---

[1] St John 10:10, *The Holy Bible*

Letter No. 26

Not My Man

Thank you for not listening to HIM. Thank you for not checking things out. Thanks for only asking but not checking it out for yourself. Thanks for falling for the okey-doke. Thank you so much for believing that lie. Since that girl from ten years ago lied, your daughter must be lying too. Besides you know your man only has eyes for you, not your 13-year-old daughter. Thanks for believing him over her because she lied last week about who she was with on the phone.

Thank you, thank you, thank you for clinging to him and not her, loving him more and her less. Thank you for putting her out and not him. Besides, you're still young. You need your man.

Thank you for not looking for her. Thank you for not taking her calls. Thanks for not caring about your grandbaby because he looks just like his daddy, your man. Thanks for finally coming around. Thank you for her new clothes. You really out did yourself with the flowers for her. Thank you for finally believing her; too bad it was too late. It was a very nice funeral.

Steal, kill, and destroy.

"Another one bites the dust. And another one gone. And another one gone. Another one bites the dust."[2]

Can't you hear the music playing in the background?

I love this song.

---

[2] Queen. The Game Album, *Another One Bites the Dust.* 1980.

Letter No. 27

Dear Old Dad

Thank you for not noticing how withdrawn she is when coming from her daddy's house. Thank you for thinking she was rejecting you, like he did. Thanks for overlooking how she played with her dolls by coloring in their eyes, cutting off their hair, and making them look as ugly as she feels.

Thank you, thank you, thank you for not listening to her when she said her pee-pee hurt. You didn't even try to see what the source of her pain was. You just dismissed it, like you were dismissed so many, many times.

Thanks for thinking how precious she was when she wanted to stay with you and not go to her dad's any more. How sweet. You never gave it a second thought; nor did you ask the doctor to check why she was bleeding. A period starts at 6? Although the bleeding did stop when she stopped visiting dear old dad, too bad the Chlamydia didn't. You didn't have a clue. Yet your disbelief is thanks enough. You're welcome.

Letter No. 28

My Boy

Thank you for needing me. Thank you for not going to church with HIM. Thank you for allowing your son to hang out with me. Thank you for not knowing who his father is. Thanks for creating that need for me to feel, I mean fill.

Thank you for not noticing his withdrawn, angry, and slightly suicidal phase. Thank you for not noticing my handprint on his face when he tried to close his jaw. Thank you for not noticing the rip in his shirt, the missing button on his jeans, or my favorite, the blood in his underwear: you did not even notice the sore on and in his mouth. Thank you so much; I always wanted a boy.

Aren't you going to congratulate me? What? No cigar? I'm so proud I have your boy. Next twins. Maybe yours.

Letter No. 29

Johnny Come Lately

Now they matter.

Now you listen.

Now you have time.

Now you take time, give time, make time.

Now HE is good.

Now you aren't caught up, in, and on anything but your baby.

Now you see her tears.

Now you see his pain.

Now it all fits.

Now you see your neglect.

Now who are you questioning? Who are you mad at? Who's really responsible? You or me?

Hey, don't feel bad. Most parents still don't change after a rape. Somehow they still make it all about them. At least you made a turnaround. Better late than never. I'm waiting. You can thank me now. And if you go back to your selfish ways, I'll be thanking you. Can you say seconds?

Letter No. 30

First of Many

Know why this book is so little? Because you can't begin to understand all my tricks. HE gave you a big book with 66 books with an old and a new testament. Y'all call it the good book and you still don't listen to HIM. HE hooked y'all up in and all around. So why should I give you a big book? Not that I can't; these few stories are nothing compared to what I do on a daily basis. This one is just about your kids. I got marriage tricks, work tricks, hell I got two books on my church tricks. All of them have the same theme - kill, steal and destroy, unlike HIM. I can have more than one book. No need to thank me, the pleasures all mine. School you later.

Cathy's Cry

Why can't they see; it's clear as day?

All she had to do was come looking for me.

Just once stop moaning and groaning about Daddy and look for me.

Why can't she smell the bleach on my breath?

Why is daddy so busy with other people's kids?

Why can't auntie notice that a 5-year-old doesn't have discharge like that in her panties?

Why can't somebody look for the baby just once?

Why am I invisible to everybody but him?

Why is bad attention better than no attention? Why?

Why can't you see my pain? Why can't you hear my cries?

Why did I have to pay for your pain with years of being your little brother's jack-off and in rag doll?

Why wasn't I loved enough to be protected from years of my little business being stretched out by someone 10 years older than me?

Why did my life have to be changed forever?

Why me?

Why was everyone blind to my pain, deaf to my silent screams, and too dumb to figure out something was really wrong with the baby?

C.W.'s Mission

My misery is now my ministry. My mission is to wake people up to pay attention and rescue any and all of our babies, and teach everyone safety awareness – parents, adults, as well as the children – everybody. It is also encouraging survivors to know:

1) There is more to you than what has happened to you

2) Living past your pain is possible

3) Silence is NOT golden in cases like these

4) God hears your silent screams and wants to comfort you

5) God cares for you and wants to heal your pain

6) Like me, you can turn your misery into your ministry

You only have to choose HIM, ask HIM, and invite HIM into your life.

C.W. Speaks – It's Time

Now Can We Talk?
If this book has hit a nerve what are you going to do? Where are you going from here? After you have screamed cried, rolled on the floor and thought about getting your gun, stop! Take stock and learn so this can stop happening. I know you know somebody else that has been forever changed by satan's workers. Who? You, your momma, your auntie, maybe even your uncle, or your brother. Are you tired yet? I'm tired, so please, please, please can we do better?

Can we do our homework on who is watching our kids?

Can we check on them even when we're tired?

Can we not trust so easily, even if it's family?

Can we pray with and over our children for God's loving protection and wisdom?

Can we not bring just any old body around our babies? (Everyone you know does not qualify to be around your babies.)

Can we stop that uncle that touched you as a child and now he wants to hold your baby girl?

Can we pay attention as if your child's life depends on it cause it does to many have killed themselves due to adults being distracted?

Are you willing to take steps to heal? For you? Your baby? Please say yes. You are worth it. Your child is worth it and the future depends on it.

If this book has made you angry, good. If anything in this book applied to you, good. If you are a parent, aunt, na na, paw paw or even an uncle and you have dropped the ball pick it up. This book was written to make you aware of just some of the schemes the devil has been pulling on us for years. It's time for it to stop. It's time for the hurt and the pain to cease. It's time to heal children, parents, siblings, aunts, uncles, and even his workers.

All of us has been played by satan. It's time for it to stop. We cannot do this in our own strength. We need GOD to guide. We need JESUS to save. We need the HOLY GHOST to comfort, and we need HIS WORD to show us the way; all day, every day, in every way. We've lost too much. We've lost too many. We've been quiet too long.

It's time to take THE LIGHT into the darkness. It's time for souls to be mended, hearts to be cleaned, and minds lined up with HIS WORD. It's time for a mass healing of the church and all its members. It's time to ask GOD for discernment on who the workers of the enemy are; so we can listen and act on what HE guides us to do. It's time out for "what happens in this house stays in this house."

It's time for the church to deal with this issue head on. I'm not just talking about the side effects of it, you know – drugs, drinking, depression, obesity, and anger. Let's not forget the many mental issues that came about from that one act that didn't only hurt the body. It scarred the mind and ripped the soul. It's time out that this major issue be taboo. No more silence. No more hush-hush. It's time to bring this dirty little secret to the light.

Let's be clear. This secret is not so little. When writing this book, I would tell people my topic and my story. So many people would say, "It happened to me," "It happened to my child," or "It happened to my mom."

No matter where I was – work, the bank, church, friends, and families –there were so many people hurting and hiding from what happened to them (or should I say they were worried that someone would find out what happened) that it frightened me. Some people are set on taking that secret to their grave. Why? Because satan has twisted things up so that the reaction of others after learning what happened is just as devastating (if not more so) than the act itself. At times it leaves the abused feeling raped, molested, or fondled all over again.

It's high time that this issue comes to light so we can wake up and pay better attention to our children. We need to create environments of awareness - not hush, hush. Let's begin the healing process, to empower our children to stand up and tell their testimony without fear of feeling raped again by judging eyes and ignorant comments. It's time.

Shepherd Speaking

John 10 - The Message

He Calls His Sheep by Name

10 ¹⁻⁵ "'Let me set this before you as plainly as I can. If a person climbs over or through the fence of a sheep pen instead of going through the gate, you know <u>he's up to no good</u>—a sheep rustler! The shepherd walks right up to the gate. The gatekeeper opens the gate to him and the sheep recognize his voice. He calls his own sheep by name and leads them out. When he gets them all out, he leads them and they follow because they are familiar with his voice. They won't follow a stranger's voice but will scatter because they aren't used to the sound of it."

⁶⁻¹⁰ Jesus told this simple story, but they had no idea what he was talking about. So he tried again. 'I'll be explicit, then. I am the Gate for the sheep. All those others are up to no good—sheep stealers, every one of them. But the sheep didn't listen to them. I am the Gate. Anyone who goes through me will be cared for—will freely go in and out, and find pasture. A thief is only there to steal and kill and destroy. I came so they can have real and eternal life, more and better life than they ever dreamed of.'

¹¹⁻¹³ 'I am the Good Shepherd. The Good Shepherd puts the sheep before himself, sacrifices himself if

necessary. A hired man is not a real shepherd. <u>The sheep mean nothing to him</u>. He sees a wolf come and runs for it, leaving the sheep to be ravaged and scattered by the wolf. He's only in it for the money. The sheep don't matter to him.'

¹⁴⁻¹⁸ 'I am the Good Shepherd. I know my own sheep and my own sheep know me. In the same way, the Father knows me and I know the Father. I put the sheep before myself, sacrificing myself if necessary. You need to know that I have other sheep in addition to those in this pen. I need to gather and bring them, too. They'll also recognize my voice. Then it will be one flock, one Shepherd. This is why the Father loves me: because I freely lay down my life. And so I am free to take it up again. No one takes it from me. I lay it down of my own free will. I have the right to lay it down; I also have the right to take it up again. I received this authority personally from my Father.'

Pick a Side

The previous passage is about tricks versus power; being taken advantage of versus being cared for. Are you willing to go in through the Gate? It all boils down to choices. Will you make the right choice? Pick a side.

God gave you the choice to belong to Him or the thief. Everything starts there. Help through this, healing from this, growing pass this pain requires God your Creator, Jesus your Savior, and the Holy Spirit your Comforter.

Salvation scripture: John 3:16 (KJV) "For God so loved the world that He gave His only begotten son that whosoever believeth in Him should not perished but have ever lasting life."

Prayer of Salvation

Dear God,

I need You to be in charge of my life. I'm buried under my sin and shame. I need You.

I believe in You sent Your Son, Jesus, through a virgin to live a sinless life to show me the way.

I believe He performed miracles so You would get the glory.

I believe He died on the cross for me.

I believe He rose on the third day with all power.

Please forgive me of all my sins.

Be the head of my life now and forever. Amen.

This book is not about blame. It is about sounding an alarm for us to wake up and pay attention. All these letters have threads of truth through them. My story is in several of the letters. I was the jack-off and in rag doll. I was the girl that didn't want anybody to tell momma. It was me having to wash my uncle's semen out of my panties. It was me who spent half of my mother's funeral in the bathroom. It was me sitting on the other side of the room to be away from that room by the repast table. It was me with PTSD. It IS me that is sick and tired of more babies not being watched, being offered up as sheep for slaughter. It's time to sound the alarm and rescue the babies. That's first and foremost!

Even when you've crossed all your T's and dotted all your I's there are circumstances when something still happens. Although those instances happen, they are not as common as when we let our guard down, get distracted, don't do our homework, don't check, trust others too easily, or think all family and friends can be trusted. Because everyone has a choice, even family and friends can make the choice to steal your trust, kill your hope, and destroy your family.

Rescue our children, sound the alarm, and create awareness to change and make the choice to heal, and not hurt. We need to extinguish any and all dangerous relationships. Release the anger to God. He has you through the anger, hate, grief, and healing process. He has you. How do I know? He had me then, and He has me still. He can work it all out for your good – if you let Him.

The fact that you have a choice to change and heal is totally up to you but this choice will affect not only you and your child but your child's future and grandchildren's future. Are you ready to break this stronghold? Are you going to let another generation go unprotected or unhealed? There are going to be temptations along the way. You must avoid any addictions: killing that fifth, hitting that blunt, pills, pills and more pills; anything that you depend on to take away the harsh reality of the situation. These things are satan at work trying to steal your focus, kill your hope, and destroy your future. Hasn't he taken enough? Haven't we all suffered at his hand enough? This will do nothing but add more mess on top of pain and too much precious time has already been wasted.

Now there is no set amount of time to this healing process, but it is a process. The key is to go through the process. At any stage you will want to park and set up camp, but don't. You are better and stronger than that.

Distractions, distractions, distractions. Distractions are satan's playground. Let's talk about distraction and all its side effects. Once I told my sister Liza if what happen to me was a cancer and was removed there would be nothing left of me. Being raped, molested, fondled as a child, and don't forget the verbal priming (talking about a child's body parts saying what you want to do to them). It saturates every fiber of our being. It fractures your soul. So many people, such as myself, are the product of distraction. You can see the side effects from the pain. It shows up as obesity, drug addictions, suicidal tendencies, alcoholism, hopelessness, depression, and many other mental issues developed to cope with the horrendously brutal acts that were done to us. In all our innocence, children are a casualty of distraction.

It was over forty years ago for me and yet it continues to happen every day to all ages, every race, religion, and financial class. Satan does not discriminate. Children are merely toys on a playground to him. It is impossible for children to know or see when they are in the middle of distraction and being set-up by satan's workers. They are helpless babies unable to see how one thing affects another and changes their life forever. Satan's thank you letters are meant to point out the obvious distractions and blind set-ups that put children in harm's way.

And then there are the hardships in life that are out of our control: sickness, death, heartbreak, change, grief, neglect, work, and depression. All these things are a part of the day-to-day issues of life that can't be changed or avoided. I didn't put that into the letters; although that too is where satan waits for that one overwhelming situation to play - stealing, killing, and destroying everyone involved. To him, overwhelming circumstances makes everything fair game. In fact, it helps him as he steals our hope, kills our joy, and destroys our will to try, live, love, believe, and trust. It's his playground. In these situations where he plays he appears to be winning - but GOD is the winner in the end, middle, and the beginning.

My Story

No one would have ever thought one mother's sickness and death would spark a change in the life of her granddaughter, her name sake - forever.

One couple from the south side of Chicago got married without a clue of what all that meant. Both husband and wife grew up poor and both in a single parent home. They had five beautiful children. But the wife's mother got sick and shortly after she passed away. Her children were devastated; three of which were young teens who had to stay with their older sister (not their father who stayed in the same city).

Of course, they all took it very hard. So hard in fact, that my mom didn't think her little brother was handling his grief by sticking his hands in the panties her 5-year-old. The only thing between him and being caught by my mom was a curtain and my silence. I wish I could say that's all that happened, and that, in and of itself was enough, but it was not.

Grief and change opened the door and heartbreak invited him in to stay awhile. My dad had no clue on how to treat my mom and she didn't know how to treat him. So, when they had big disagreements my mom was off, gone to vent to her sisters in Chicago, from Chicago to Detroit and back. She didn't know her brother had graduated from using his hands to full penetration with nothing between us but my sister's nylon panties - because they were bigger. So, at every visit he allowed satan to use him to make me his jack off, in and on rag from the ages to 5 to almost 9.

In Chicago, my dad was not there. And when my uncle came to visit us in Detroit, my dad was busy at his new job. My siblings were not around because, as the youngest, my mom would only take me to Chicago. And when they were around, they didn't know either. They were young too. Even when he asked my sister to "Let me wear your panties," it didn't click. My aunt didn't think when she made me wash my panties. "Surely," she thought, I was a "pissy-tail little girl that played too much." If she had known she was making me clean my uncle's semen out of my panties, she would have beat the black off him.

Often it is not one thing, it's layers of issues that surround a child leaving him or her unprotected. Our distractions are satan's playground every day like life, death, change, heartbreak, or a new job. Satan takes great strides during those situations to come in through any cracks that distraction reveals.

Let's take a panoramic view of the source of my pain; the one event that changed the very fabric of my soul.

My grandmother passed away – but death is a part of life.

My parents had their troubles – what marriage doesn't.

My aunt's grief plus caring for three teenagers – that's hard on anyone.

My siblings never had a clue and never thought it. No one would've ever thought that the baby was being molested.

My mom's broken heart put me in harm's way – she had no idea.

My dad's new job with all the stress that brings – he just didn't know.

My uncle loses his mom, goes to live with his sister - not his Dad who lived in the same city, not to mention he was young, dumb, and easily influenced by satan's tricks.

And then last but not least – there's me. I was just a baby; the baby who was invisible – except to him. Yes, my young uncle was working for satan at such a young age. Satan preys on the vulnerable, not only his victims or should I say his quests, but also his minions and his workers – all of the above. Since the time of Adam and Eve he has and will do his job to kill, steal, and destroy – but God is able to heal and change the hearts and minds of both victim and perpetrator.

Only GOD

"I came so they can have real and eternal life, more and better life than they ever dreamed of."   John 10:10 MSG

Only God can take a couple with no clue through the death of a child and parents, new jobs, old jobs, some money, no money, and have a stressed out marriage that withstood the hardship of life for 50 years – only God.

Only God healed my mother and her siblings from losing their mother, their rock, their Ma Dear.

Only God gave my aunt strength to take in her siblings with the hole in her heart from losing her mother – only God.

Only God kept my siblings and me as we endured the hardships that growing up brings, because they all had their own issues from our parents' distractions. But God has kept us all – we are all saved by His grace and mercy.

Only God kept my mother and her siblings through the pains of grief and life and all are saved by His grace as well – yes, my uncle too.

Only God kept and helped me when I wanted to die by my own hands.

Only God held me in His arms when I spent weekends in my closet having memory after memory all the while feeling like it was happening for the first time. Every nasty account that should have fractured my mind when it scarred my soul.

Only God kept me through the verbal, mental, and physical abuse that started right when the sexual abuse stopped.

Only God saw me when I was invisible to everyone – except my uncle.

Only God kept me from ripping my family apart so that today I can be the voice He would have me to be.

Only God kept me at my mother's funeral that was held at one of the many places my uncle abused me – in the basement of the church in the room by the repast table (although for 50% of the service I was in the bathroom).

Only God kept me after losing my Fanny. She was my best friend and my mother. She was the one person that I protected though I remained unprotected.

Only God knows all my dark, deep pains that I cannot even mention, and He loves me still.

Only God gave me the will to live, love, and still joke and smile through it all.

Only God can remove all my bitterness, anger, and pain.

Only God protected me from myself after my mom died. I thought she was the only reason I didn't hurt my uncle like he hurt me – but it was God.

Only God can take me, a product of distraction, through the grace of not remembering what happened until I was 16, with all of its pain in order to endure the process of healing; to want to be the voice of those who have suffered in silence from childhood sexual abuse.

Only GOD was with me when I spent weekends in my closet so I could feel safe in my first apartment.

Only GOD knows our hurts and our sins and delivers us from them all

Only God kept me from tearing up my family, because I was angry at them all.

Only God kept me from slitting my wrist in my college bathroom when life got to be a bit too much.

Only God kept my brother who wanted to tell, scream, and fight. God stopped him from hurting my uncle and from telling my secret when I was just not ready for the world to know.

Only God healed me when I didn't ever want to trust the group of people that I called family who had hurt me the most.

Only God guided my husband to love and protect the five-year-old girl inside me, although satan's tricks corrupted that union.

Only God protected my girls when I would panic because they stayed in the church bathroom two minutes too long.

Only God removed the bitterness in my heart and the "Why me?" from my mind and replaced it with forgiveness and assurance that He will work it all out for my good.

Only God took me from being a statistic to being a published author, evangelist, advocate, and speaker.

Only God gave me the strength to forgive and the wisdom to ask for forgiveness.

Only God knows how deep rooted my pain is, and He is the only one that can continue to heal me through it all.

Only God has kept me from throwing my hands up because there are too many hurting people for me to handle. Only God, in all His patience, let me know it's Him doing all the handling – not me.

Only God sends people to me so I can give them to Him. It's simply a catch and release. It's not about me. It's all about Him and His wisdom, strength, and power.

Only God birthed this book out of my anger and pain after I found out that my favorite was raped by a close family friend; when I really wanted to catch a case.

Only God saved my uncle which was difficult for me to accept. This is the ultimate truth – HE sent His son to die for me (the abused) and my uncle (the abuser). That fact, that truth has taken me years of growing and healing to accept and all I don't understand, only God, my God can help me with that too.

Only God came that we might have life, and that we might have it more abundantly.

Only God can help you through your pains too.

Only God…

GOD's Love Letter

There will never be a time that satan will have the last say. I will always have the last say just like I had the first. I AM the Alpha and Omega, the beginning and the end. I will always have the large H, just like he will always have the small h. I love you. I know all your hurts, pains, and troubles. I AM with them in the closet crying. I AM with them through all their triggers. I know they feel alone. I know they're angry at Me, their parents, family, and friends. On this side everyone has a choice. The choice to follow him or Me.

A person that hurts others has a choice, and when they choose him, they will get their due with him. But now you have a choice to come to Me with all your anger, worries, fears, hurt, and pain. I love you so much that I gave my only begotten Son that whosoever (that's you) believes in Me should not perish but will have everlasting life.

Satan has been manipulating people since Adam and Eve. Just as I have been merciful, forgiving, and giving grace that is new every morning. Stop take a minute to understand your part in all of this. You may be one of the ones that have been hurt; or maybe you're a worker; or you may be an adult in a child's life. Are you protecting them, or are you too caught up in your own life? Do you filter who comes into the child's life or do you need to check yourself and change. It's not too late to change.

If it has not happened to you, thank Me (God) and ask for discernment. If it has happened repent (if you are saved) and ask that child to forgive you. If you are not saved and you choose to be, you must believe that Jesus came from a virgin, lived a sinless life, performed miracles so that God could get the glory, died for all your sins, and arose from the dead after three days with all power in His hands. He has gone to prepare a place for all who believe. Ask Me (God) to forgive you of all your sins and ask Jesus to come into your heart, mind, body, and soul.

It's your choice to heal and forgive, and to protect and watch over all the children I have blessed you to care for. Find comfort in My words.

~ ~ ~

Matthew 18 (KJV)

"¹ At the same time came the disciples unto Jesus, saying, Who is the greatest in the kingdom of heaven?

² And Jesus called a little child unto him, and set him in the midst of them,

³ And said, Verily I say unto you, Except ye be converted, and become as little children, ye shall not enter into the kingdom of heaven.

⁴ Whosoever therefore shall humble himself as this little child, the same is greatest in the kingdom of heaven.

⁵ And whoso shall receive one such little child in my name receiveth me.

⁶ But whoso shall offend one of these little ones which believe in me, it were better for him that a millstone were hanged about his neck, and that he were drowned in the depth of the sea.

⁷ Woe unto the world because of offences! for it must needs be that offences come; but woe to that man by whom the offence cometh!"

1 Peter 5:6-8 (KJV)

"⁶ Humble yourselves therefore under the mighty hand of God, that he may exalt you in due time:

⁷ Casting all your care upon him; for he careth for you.

⁸ Be sober, be vigilant; because your adversary the devil, as a roaring lion, walketh about, seeking whom he may devour:"

1 John 3:8b (KJV)

"⁸ᵇ For this purpose the Son of God was manifested, that he might destroy the works of the devil."

Romans 8:34b-39 (KJV)

"³⁴ᵇ it is Christ that died, yea rather, that is risen again, who is even at the right hand of God, who also maketh intercession for us.

³⁵ Who shall separate us from the love of Christ? shall tribulation, or distress, or persecution, or famine, or nakedness, or peril, or sword?

³⁶ As it is written, For thy sake we are killed all the day long; we are accounted as sheep for the slaughter.

³⁷ Nay, in all these things we are more than conquerors through him that loved us.

³⁸ For I am persuaded, that neither death, nor life, nor angels, nor principalities, nor powers, nor things present, nor things to come,

³⁹ Nor height, nor depth, nor any other creature, shall be able to separate us from the love of God, which is in Christ Jesus our Lord."

~ ~ ~

Through all your pain, fear, loneliness, no matter what was done to you or what you've done. I AM the way the truth and the light.

I love you.

I was given this prayer that I believe is just for you and whatever you're going through.

~ ~ ~

Precious Blood Prayer

My Dearest Jesus, I plead Your precious blood over my mind, my body, my emotions, my nervous system, my thoughts, my feelings, and my imagination, and I ask You to give me Your wonderful peace that only You can give, that nothing or no one else can give, but only You, please bless me and my family in a very special way. During this time, Jesus, I thank You for Your loving care. I thank You that You are always with me, because You said that You will never leave me nor forsake me, and I stand on that promise because I know that You always keep Your promises.

I praise You. I love You. I worship You, and I give You all the glory. I ask one more thing, dear Jesus, that You be my strength, my hope, my joy, and my everything. Amen.

About the Author

Former silent sufferer C. W. Fossett is on a mission to serve as an abuse advocate who speaks for the silent sufferers of childhood sexual abuse who have not yet spoken for themselves.

Promoting awareness to protect our precious children through Precious Butterfly Ministries she teaches youth how to protect themselves, it's safe to tell, and that it's okay to say "NO!"

Using her motivational, straight forward, and humorous style of speaking, she seeks to motivate survivors to know that Jesus came to heal the brokenhearted, blind, and bruised so that they can have life past their pain. That abundant life, C.W. teaches, is provided through the love and care of the Good Shepherd Jesus Christ.

C.W. Fossett holds a Bachelor's Degree from Marygrove College, is the proud mother of two, doting grandmother of three and lives in Detroit, Michigan.

BOOK ORDER FORM

Thanks for Everything!
By C.W. Fossett

Name _____

Address _____

City _____ State _____ Zip _____

Phone _____ Fax _____

Email _____

Quantity	
Price *(each)*	$10.99
Subtotal	
S & H *(each)*	$1.99
MI Tax 6%	
TOTAL	

METHOD OF PAYMENT:

☐ Check or Money Order (*Make payable to*: C. W. Fossett)

☐ Visa ☐ Master Card ☐ American Express

Acct No. _____

Expiration Date (*mmyy*) _____

Signature _____

Mail your payment with this form to:
C.W. Fossett
c/o PriorityONE Publications
P.O. Box 34722
Detroit, MI 48234
(313) 312-5318
URL: http://www.cwfossett.com
Email: info@cwfossett.com

www.ingramcontent.com/pod-product-compliance
Lightning Source LLC
Chambersburg PA
CBHW071537080526
44588CB00011B/1705